I0470611

100 More Ways to
Boost Your Creativity

A Guide For Visual Artists Working In
Two Dimensions

Lisa Mayfield

100 More Ways to Boost Your Creativity: A Guide for Visual Artists Working In Two Dimensions

© Copyright 2013 by Lisa Mayfield. All rights reserved.

Published by Wandering Bard Press at CreateSpace

ISBN: 978-1484904046

100 More Ways to Boost Your Creativity

A Guide For Visual Artists
Working In Two Dimensions

Thank you for purchasing this short but powerful guide. My name is Lisa Mayfield, and in just a few minutes, I guarantee that you will find something here that will spark an idea and get those creative juices flowing. By following just a few of these suggestions, you will be able to bust through a creative block, begin creating more work, and have more ideas than ever before. I have used these techniques myself, and they will work for you, too. If you follow some of these suggestions, prompts and ideas, your creative flow will increase in both quantity and quality.

But first, you need to understand a few things.

Thing 1: This is not a dissertation on the creative process, nor is it presenting anything new. All of this material may be found around the Internet, in books, and through attendance at a variety of conferences, workshops and classes. What I have done here is to condense it down into the information you need in order to boost your creativity now, and to get the results you want, faster and more efficiently than before.

Thing 2: There are many, many writers and teachers out there who understand what creativity is, and how to teach others to tap into their creative potential. I have been a student at their collective table since I was very young, and now I invite you to learn what I have learned over many, many years as a Creative.

Thing 3: There is very little in this book that repeats the information found in my first book, "60 Ways to Boost Your Creativity". The suggested activities in this book are all new, as well as the "Year of Creativity Project" section. So really, that only leaves the next sections, "What is Creativity"and "What is the Creative Process", as a rerun.

What is Creativity?

Unfortunately, very few people truly understand the meaning of the word "creative". Most think it's synonymous with the word "artistic", and that you must have some innate or learned artistic talent or skill, or even a degree in traditional media and artistic techniques. That's hogwash.

Creativity is not "artistic skill". It is the ability to solve a problem. When a painter sits to paint a landscape, she's not just painting a picture of what she sees (either in front of her or in her mind's eye); she's trying to solve a problem. Perhaps the problem is, "How do I use these paints to represent this scene as accurately as possible?" Or perhaps she wants to imitate the style of a well-known artist, like Matisse, or Van Gogh. No matter. She has a goal. She wants to put what is in her head on the canvas or paper.

People who believe they have little or no "artistic skill" solve problems every day. For example, a computer programmer is creative if she writes a program to accomplish a task. She may not be able to draw a stick figure very well, but she is still "creative" because she is able to use what she knows to come up with a novel solution to the problem at hand. If the solution weren't novel, she would simply have used a previously created code snippet to perform the function, and moved on. Or consider the medical researcher, who is trying to come up with a new treatment that will be both effective and safe for some specific medical condition. Again, if the goal is to solve a problem, the person solving the problem is engaged in the creative process.

So, if the Creative is an artist trying to break out of a bout of doldrums, where the creative vibe simply isn't happening, that's a problem. And, like all such problems, it can be solved. Perhaps not easily or quickly, but the solution is there waiting.

Oh, and by the way, when I use the word "Creative" with a capital "C", I'm talking about people who consider themselves to be creative thinkers (and doers), those who routinely come up with ideas to solve problems. When I use the same word with a lower case "c", I'm talking about the description of the type of activity that leads to new ideas and solutions to problems.

What is the Creative Process?

Creatives often understand the creative process instinctively, just as a young athlete who seems "gifted" at her sport has an innate ability to push her body to improve her performance. Creativity can be taught, nurtured, improved upon or even dismissed, depending on how an individual chooses to see herself, and how those around her see her.

Believe it or not, most people are born with the innate ability to create at will; even, some might argue, the need to do so. Picture, if you will, a small child who happens to get hold of a tube of toothpaste, and begins smearing it around all over the bathroom floor and cabinets, then beams proudly at her masterpiece. She isn't just creating a mess; she's making art with the materials at hand.

If a person sees a problem, any problem, and comes up with a way to solve that problem, some people in her circle of influence may see her as a "problem solver", while others may see her as a "dreamer", or "distracted", or even as a "meddler". Depending on whether she accepts any of these labels, she may feel encouraged to solve more problems, or she may turn into a wallflower who never offers solutions when presented with a problem.

In school, we are typically taught that there is only one correct answer to any problem. But Creatives know better; there may literally be hundreds of ways to solve any given problem. Many of those ways, however, may not be feasible given the constraints of cost, time or the laws of physics. So the list of plausible solutions is reduced to a fraction of the possible solutions, and reduced again, and possibly again, until one solution is found to fit best among the choices, and within the given constraints.

The creative process is a series of internal planning stages a Creative goes through to solve a problem. Often, these steps or stages are completed subconsciously, and the Creative has no conscious knowledge of how they were accomplished. In fact, the process may appear to the Creative like this: A, B, J, Z! Often, these leaps look to others as though there is no logic, no progression from point to point. The truth is that Creatives often make these leaps more quickly, without the need to follow the progression step-by-step. The trouble comes in when trying to explain the thought process to others who were not privy to the thoughts themselves.

Ideally, the "problem" is broken down into steps, parts or components. Once the pieces are solved, the problem can be solved. If this step is ignored, the solution is not likely to be complete, and most likely will not work in the end.

As an example, an artist may plan a painting by starting with the background and working toward the front, layer by layer, seeing what is behind the subject and setting up the painting of the foreground last. Some artists, however, would paint the main subject first, then add the background layer later, almost as an afterthought. Which method is better? Whatever works for the artist.

Have you ever taken a photograph that you just KNEW would make a stunning print, only to get the print back (or open it in your photo editor) and realize that you never noticed the power lines in the background, or the clutter in the foreground, or the guy off to one side who just happened to walk into the frame as you clicked the shutter? Why didn't you notice those things before? Because you weren't *seeing* them. Your eyes saw them, but your brain was focused on some other aspect of the shot, and didn't register the problem areas. Now the problem becomes "How do I fix this?" And that's where the Creative would go to work.

I've heard it said that Ansel Adams never sold a photograph straight from the negative that came out of his camera. He always custom-printed each photograph, burning and dodging each one so the finished print would match how he saw the original scene in his mind's eye. If you were to print directly from his original negatives, without adjustments, I doubt the finished prints would be very impressive. This is what takes an artistic work from "technically good" to "creatively and artistically amazing".

The Year of Creativity Project

On January 1, 2013, I began what I had hoped would become a weekly feature on my blog: "The Year of Creativity Project". I had intended to post one creative project each week, figuring that I could find the time in my hectic life to create and post 52 projects in a year. That doesn't sound too hard, does it?

I was shocked – then amazed – at the results! From the first day, I found more ideas, and at a faster rate, than ever before! My biggest trouble was finding the time to make everything I found bursting forth from my subconscious – er, my Muse. Some days, especially any day I didn't have to go to work, I found myself creating several separate projects in a single day.

How did this happen? My best guess is that, once I had made the concious decision to **allow** myself the time to be creative, my Muse jumped for joy, then started digging around and working overtime to provide me with bucketsful of ideas to work into my projects.

Some days I came home from my day job, exhausted and cranky from a long drive home, ate a quick bite of dinner with the family, then went up to my office where I doodled on the computer for a few minutes until I had something with which I was satisfied enough to post. On those days, an interesting thing happened: I was more relaxed and happier by the time I had finished than I was when I started, no matter how the project turned out, or how long it took.

Over the next several months, I began paying

attention to my moods and thoughts before and after creating some sort of work of art. Many days, even though I was a little frustrated that my attempts to copy the picture in my head did not live up to the original concept, instead of feeling frustration, I was able to simply let the final work be its own creation. I was able to accept my "failure" (as an artist) as simply another direction where I could learn more skills, if I chose to put my energy into that effort.

And I moved on.

This amazed me, since I tend to hold to perfectionism and expecting "more" of myself. I expect my first efforts to be expert quality, with no need for that thing called a "learning curve". I expect to have the talent and skill to do whatever I'm attempting, first time, every time.

I expect not to fail.

This was who I was before that January 1. Since then, I have learned that I don't want or need to be a perfect artist in every medium or with every topic or subject I'm trying to depict with my projects.

I don't need to be perfect. At anything.

It's OK to fail.

It's OK to decide I don't like a particular technique or medium.

It's OK to continue using a particular technique or medium over and over and over again, until I'm ready to do something different.

Between January 1, and April 10, the first 100 days in

my Year of Creativity, I learned many important lessons. Here is a sampling:

- **Art is in the eye of the beholder.** Oh, I've known this for many years. But always before, I *cared* what other people thought of my work. This time, I'm not showing it online to receive accolades or even acknowledgement. I'm posting my work to keep myself accountable to the project. As a Creative, if I say it's art, then it's art.

- **Anyone can be creative.** Some people have to create all day long for their jobs. Photographers, graphic designers, fashion designers, web designers, writers, illustrators, painters, sculptors, fiber artists, composers, choreographers, advertising executives, book designers, magazine editors, landscapers, architects, computer programmers, chefs, bloggers… The list is pretty much endless. Most people go through their day not understanding that just about everyone can turn their day job or their spare time into a more creative endeavor. To paraphrase a famous quote, "Whether you think you can create, or think you can't, either way, you're right."

- **Becoming a Creative is more a matter of deciding *that* you will create, rather than any inherent talent or learned skill.** Neither Leonardo DaVinci, Michelangelo, Georgia O'Keefe, nor any other painter you care to name painted a masterpiece the first time they touched a brush. Each had to learn the basics, and practice endlessly, for *years*, to learn and perfect their craft. Oh, and by the way, none of these three was just a painter. All three artists pursued other creative endeavors as well. True enough, you must start with the *will* to create.

After that, creating is simply a matter of doing what you love. Over and over and over again. Whether you feel like it or not.

- **Give yourself permission to fail.** This is such an important concept, I'll say it again. **Give yourself permission to fail.** Not every idea will work out the way you hope or expect. And one day, it may work out even better than you had planned. The trick is to not get too disappointed with (or attached to) your results. Try again. Try a different way. Try something else. Go on to something different, or go for a long walk or a drive. Leave it alone. Let your subconscious work it out. Then go for it (whatever "it" ends up becoming).

- **Yoda was wrong.** Yoda said, "Do or do not. There is no try." That's just a bunch of hooey. There **is** try, as long as you don't let one failure (or two, or three…) make you quit. It's the only way anything new is created.

- **Yoda was right.** OK, I hear you all now: "Wait, you just said he was wrong." That's right, I did. But then again, what he could have meant was this: "If you want to be creative, then create. Don't just 'try' to create, because if you just 'try' and you don't succeed at your first attempt, you'll quit." You can't "wish" your creativity into existence. You must create. You must **make stuff**. If you want to be a writer, then you must write. If you want to be a painter, then you must paint. If you want to be a chef, then you must cook. If all you ever do with your ideas is dream about them becoming reality, you're not a Creative, you're a Dreamer. You are the one who must make the dreams real.

- **Listen to your Muse.** Your Muse can speak to

you in any number of ways, at any time of day or night. You have to be ready to hear her whispers (or, in my case, take the beatings over the head). She will give you ideas if you invite her to speak to you. Maybe not right away, but she **will** come. Be ready once she does. Have some way of noting the ideas as they arrive, even if you're not able to stop what you're doing and act on them. Write a quick note. Send yourself an email. Leave yourself a voice mail. Sketch it out on the back of an envelope. Write it on your hand. If you keep a small notebook with you, that could help you remember when inspiration whispers in your ear. Or whacks you on the back of the head.

- **Set time aside.** If you create better when you are alone, set some alone time. Make an appointment with yourself, and keep it. If you create better in collaboration with others, find a willing partner or group to get together on a regular basis to create *en masse*. Put the appointment on your calendar, or make a commitment to yourself that, no matter what, you will take the time you need to create. Follow my example, and make a commitment to create something every day, even if you're not thrilled with what you have created.

- **Creatives *must* create.** If you want to be a Creative, you must first get into the mindset of a Creative. Creatives *must* create, or they die a little inside their own psyches. I've known many Creatives who become cranky little jerks when they are not able to exercise their creativity (yes, that includes me).

- **Creativity is really just problem-solving.** Even if you think you can't draw a decent stick figure, if you solve problems well, then you are already a Creative. Creatives solve problems all the time. Composers try to elicit a mood, emotion or image, or set their own or some else's words to music (or vice versa). Painters try to capture an image or emotion with their chosen medium on their chosen surface. Sometimes a Creative is paid to come up with ideas and render them on a daily, or hourly, basis. Sometimes the "problem" becomes "what next?"

- **The more ideas you come up with, the better and more novel the ideas become.** Just like practicing the piano, when you practice the art of developing ideas, you get better at it. It's like building a muscle. It takes time and practice, but it does get easier, and you can do it faster and better the more you do it.

- **If you don't know what you want to do, try lots of different things.** Sometimes the process of executing an idea proves to you that this is not really the direction in which you want to take your creative energies. Try something else. Try lots of things. Sometimes the technique you're trying is related to a different technique that you may find comes easier to you. Sometimes something totally unrelated "clicks" for you. If nothing has clicked yet, keep going. It's out there, waiting for you. Trust me. I've recently read someone else's blog, where she called this "hopscotch" - hopping from one idea, project or technique to another. Personally, I don't see the problem with this. I enjoy the diversity of experience!

- **Focus is good.** If you decide you want to be a world-famous manga artist, work at it like you're training for a triathlon. Do it every day. Improve your basic skills. Show your work to others who enjoy manga, and get their opinions on what you need to do to improve even more. There's nothing wrong with becoming a "one-trick pony". Many photographers will never try sculpture or writing. Many poets will never pick up a camera. Find your "thing", then do it. A lot. Keep on doing it. Have fun with it. Stretch, explore, and play. If it becomes a chore, you may want to give it up. It should be challenging, but in a good way. And once you get the basics down, stretch some more. Keep improving and growing as a Creative.

- **Having fun with your creative pursuits will help you improve even more.** It's hard to put a lot of energy into a task that isn't fun. Example: I don't enjoy housework. At. All. I don't like to cook much, or clean, or pretty much do anything having to do with keeping a tidy home. It isn't fun to me. Neither is running. But let me sit in front of my computer or sewing machine with good music playing and several hours to play, and I'm in heaven. I have worked at many creative pursuits during my lifetime: weaving, spinning yarn, dyeing fibers and fabric, sewing, quilting, costume and jewelry design, painting, sculpture, ceramics, writing, photography, digital art, web design, and more. Whenever a particular craft became boring or stopped being fun, I quit doing it for a while. So, it doesn't matter what method, technique or medium you choose, or how many of them you choose: if you enjoy a particular craft, do it as much as you are able.

- **You are not what you do.** No matter what anyone else will tell you, you are not your job. Your identity can be as fluid as you like. You can identify yourself as a Creative, currently working in such-and-such industry or with so-and-so employment status, if you want. When I was a stay-at-home mom, I would often tell people I was "Chief Operations Officer of a small, family-run enterprise." In fact, I wrote up an entire executive résumé based on the many tasks that a SAHM is required to perform in a given day, week, month or year of taking care of a home and family. That exercise was creative and fun, plus it gave my ego a boost to know that I was capable of performing executive-level management duties (at least on paper), in addition to running after little kids, changing diapers, and listening to Barney for hours on end.

- **If you think the sky is the limit, you're thinking too small.** To a Creative, the universe is the limit. Think of all the Creatives employed in the Space Exploration industry. They have to design a spacecraft that will withstand the extremes of space travel, and continue to function and return signals for years without further human intervention. Or the engineers who designed and maintain the International Space Station, with its frequent flights of various spacecraft to resupply the ISS and transport crews safely between Earth and the ISS. What is creating a new piece of digital art compared with that task?!

- **Internal inspiration can be far more powerful than external inspiration.** The ideas that are generated within your mind can produce a far more intense reaction than any instruction from any outside source. Think back to any course you took in high school or college. If you took the class because it was a requirement to graduate, and not because you had any innate desire or interest in the subject, you probably spent less time and energy on the work for the class. If, however, you took a class primarily because of your interest (perhaps as an elective), you were probably more excited, and likely enjoyed your projects and assignments more as a result. Perhaps you even got better grades for those courses. When you are interested in learning more about a subject, your focus shifts to that topic. Everything else seems to fade off into the distance.

- **When you're blocked, just make something. Anything.** When you experience a creative "block", you're likely having a moment of doubt or fear that any idea you come up with will not be "good enough". That's ok. Just make up some silly little something while you're waiting for your Muse to get back to you. Doodle. Draw a cartoon, or an "ugly" picture. Write a stupid limerick, or a poem that doesn't make sense. Go for a walk, then come back and write or draw nonsense. Eventually, you should feel a nudge, or hear a whisper, or see the fog begin to lift. And the more often you do this, the quicker the fog will lift.

- **Curiosity is a Creative's best friend.** Creatives often ask, "What if…" This is the most important question ever asked by any human. In fact, it's probably the only question that ever led to the solution of any problem ever in the history of humankind.

- **It's ok to wait until another day.** Unless you make your living by solving problems at the speed of demand, you don't have to make art every day. Or every other day. Take your time. Read or watch or see or touch or hear or smell or taste or do something inspirational. Or just go for a walk. Or sit under a tree for an hour. Or listen to the ocean wash onto the shore. Close your eyes and **listen**. It's there, whispering to you, but sometimes the noise in your life, or just inside your own head, is drowning it out. Be still, and it will come. But don't use a short "break" as an excuse to give up!

- **Don't panic!** If you're having trouble coming up with ideas, don't panic. Breathe deeply and slowly. Close your eyes. Relax. Feel your pulse slow. Let go of the fear. Smile and keep breathing. And bring a towel.

- **You bring your own reality.** When you say things like "I can't" and "I'm not", then you make it so. Instead, try saying things like "I've never tried it before" or "I might be able to", then go ahead and give it a try. But don't quit just because your first attempt didn't bring you the results you wanted. Take a deep breath, and try again. Keep practicing.

- **Start with something simple.** When you're trying something new, start with the basics, the simple stuff. If the simple stuff comes easily, progress to the next step, then the next, until you can do the master-level work. Have you ever seen true art made with crayons? It's amazing! That is mastery of a craft! And it all started with the silliest scribbles of a toddler who was more likely to eat the crayon than to ever make master-level art with it.

- **There's a reason we use the word "inspiration" to mean both the internal nudge that helps us to create, and taking in a breath.** When you are having trouble producing ideas, you need to remember to breathe deeply and consciously. Breathe in and out, slowly and rhythmically, and listen for the inner voice that will bring you hints and clues to help you solve your problem. Richard Bach wrote, "There is no such thing as a problem without a gift for you in its hands. You seek problems because you need their gifts." The gifts they bring are often creative solutions which others can then use to solve their problems.

Prompts

Sometimes we just need a little "something" to get our creative juices going, but we're not quite sure where to start. Or we just want someone – *anyone* – to tell us what to do next. We can't decide among the thousands of possibilities (OK, the possibilities are really infinite, but I didn't think that would help you just now), and we just want someone else to decide for us.

Well, today's your lucky day! Let me decide for you. I'll show you how easy it is.

But before we get started, let me make a suggestion: use a pen or marker, so you won't be tempted to correct any "mistakes". With these exercises, there's no such thing as a mistake. Make your marks, and move on. Use unintentional marks to decorate, embellish and enhance your drawing. You might just surprise yourself with how much you can come up with when you try this.

1. Draw a set of circles. Make some concentric, others overlapping, and still others separate. Fill them however you like.

2. Draw a set of triangles, but make sure that no two have the same angles. Make some short and fat, others tall and thin, some with each side a different length, some equilateral. Overlap some, put smaller ones inside larger ones, leave some separated from the rest. Fill in the shapes however you like.

3. Draw several 4-sided shapes, with no two exactly the same. Use squares of different sizes,

rectangles of different dimensions, rhomboids, parallelograms, trapezoids. Arrange them in any way that seems right to you. Fill in the shapes.

4. Draw two heavy, straight lines that meet at some random angle you choose. Pick a measurement, such as 1/8 inch, or 5 mm, and place a dot at each such point along your lines. Use a straight edge of some sort, and draw lines to connect the dots from one heavy line to the other. Starting at the end of one line, connect to the dot on the other line closest to where the two lines meet. Continue around until you've used as many dots as possible. Use different colors, if you like.

5. Using 3 or more thick, straight lines, follow the instructions in prompt #4. Decide whether you want your lines to meet at the ends, cross, or float separately. Each choice will produce a different result.

6. Write your name (or someone else's), or any other word of your choice in cursive. Turn the paper around and make a mirror image of the word. Decorate the image however you like, using colors, embellishments, loops, spikes, halos, wings, or anything else you wish.

7. Draw a non-linguistic symbol of your choice. Make it as large or small as you like. Make one or many, overlapping or separate. Add any kind of embellishment you like. Play with it. Disguise it until only you know what you started out with.

8. I mentioned Zentangles in my previous book. This is an excellent technique for playing with shape and line. If you search the Internet for "Enthusiastic Artist" or go directly to enthusiasticartist.blogspot.com, you will find a

wealth of samples and tutorials on how to create some amazing patterns. If you'd prefer to start with the basics, you can find dozens of books at Amazon.com with instructions for basic, intermediate and advanced designs. Try some of the basics, just filling in the 4-inch space as recommended by the creators, then do the "tangling" inside random framing shapes.

9. Design the perfect bathroom. It doesn't have to be like a painting. It can be just a sketch, with a floor plan and boxes for what goes where. Add whatever amenities you like. Make it as big as you like. Design the color scheme, materials, finishes. Remember, money is no object! Think outside the box. Just because it's a bathroom doesn't mean it can only have bathroom-like items in it...

10. Design the perfect office. Use the same concepts as in #9. Size is no object. Money is no object. Location is no object.

11. Design a guitar. Use any theme, any materials, and any color scheme you like. Remember, it must still be playable! Either electric or acoustic, or a combination if you prefer.

12. Design a treehouse. This can be for a child, an adult, or a family. Decide what sort of rooms and furnishings you would like, and select colors and materials for decorating.

13. Draw a scene from the most recent dream you can remember having. If you don't remember your dreams, ask someone to describe their dream to you and draw it.

14. Without looking at a mirror, photograph, or any other image or camera, draw your own face. Be as detailed as you like. Show the

drawing to someone who knows you well, and ask them who it is.

15. Put your hand on a piece of paper, fingers spread apart, and trace around your entire hand and wrist. Turn the tracing into something that is NOT a hand.

16. Make a "No Solicitors" sign for the front door to your home. You can be as nice or as mean as you like with it.

17. Start your "bucket list" - a list of things you'd like to do before you "kick the bucket". But don't write it down – draw it! Make your list as large or small as you like, but include as much detail as possible.

18. What do you fear most in the world? Draw it. Make it as detailed as you can stand. Then write in large letters across the paper affirmations like, "I am not my fear," or "I am stronger than my fear."

19. Or make the drawing of your worst fear very, very tiny, on a large piece of paper, and surround it with drawings of things you love so they overpower the tiny little thing you fear.

20. What do you love most in the world? Draw it. Make it as detailed as you can. Fill the page with images of what you love. It can be anything or anyone. Just be honest.

21. Draw a "pleasure pavilion". Whatever that means to you. Make it as detailed as possible.

22. Draw a Western scene. Whatever that means to you. Make it as detailed as possible.

23. Draw a stiletto. Knife or shoe (or something else), your choice.

24. Draw a scene or item that depicts the phrase, "Better than ever!" Fill the image with emotion.

25. Draw a scene or item that depicts the word "disgust". Fill the image with emotion.

26. Draw a scene, item or symbol that depicts the word "hatred". Fill the image with emotion.

27. Create a new money system. Use coins, bills, tokens, or any other system you choose. It should make sense, and be easy to use for anyone who has trouble with math or with vision.

28. Create a new money system, but make it as complex as you like. Next, make a competing money system, complete with exchange rates that fluctuate based on some arbitrary basis, such as day of week, or moon phase, or somebody rolling some dice. Make at least some of your competing denominations look similar in size, shape and color (but have totally different values, of course), just to confuse matters.

29. Draw an image depicting your idea of "the beach". Be as detailed as possible. If you hate the beach, make it as horrible as possible; if you love it, make it as wonderful as possible.

30. Draw an underwater city. Make it as detailed as possible.

Larger Project Ideas

Rather than using a different prompt each day/week/choose-your-interval, how about starting a larger project, something that will sustain you for several weeks, months, or even an entire year? You are free to choose your medium, whether it is crayon, colored pencil, markers, chalk, conté crayon, watercolor, acrylic, oil, or pixels (to include digital photography), or any other colored medium you care to use. If you use a digital medium (aka "pixels"), you can easily upload your finished images to your blog or website. If you use other media, you will need to scan or photograph the finished piece before you will be able to put it online.

Post your results to a blog (lots of free blogs are available at wordpress.com, blogspot.com or dozens of other free blog sites online) or to your own website. If you don't have access to the internet or a computer, use a Creativity Journal instead. Then find one or more people to share your creations with.

1. Start your own "Year of Creativity Project". Select one day a week (or one hour each day, if you're feeling inspired) and designate it "Creativity Day" (or "Creativity Time"), and give yourself the gift of creativity. Start it on whatever day you wish. You don't have to wait for January 1! Put it on your calendar, and mark it as "Very Important!" Do not skip the appointment unless it is absolutely vital that you do. Make whatever your Muse tells you to make. If you are struggling for ideas, use one or more of the prompts in the previous section. If you'd like, follow the suggestions in #2 below, and choose a theme for your project.

2. Select a theme (e.g. "Valentine's Day Every

Day"), a subject (e.g. "nature"), or any other criteria you choose. Stick to this theme on whatever schedule you choose. Create a series of images related to this one theme/subject/whatever. Should a different idea strike you, do that in addition to your regularly scheduled piece. Feel free to start a secondary project.

3. Create a major arcana tarot deck (22 cards) using your own symbolism and images. Create each drawing in only 5 minutes. Or take 15 minutes to do each drawing (or an hour, if you prefer), but do one each day (or each week) until you're done.

4. Select one suit of the minor arcana tarot cards, and create the entire set of 14 cards by making one each day for two weeks. Use whatever symbolism and imagery you like.

5. Create a new deck of playing cards (poker-type). Create new images/symbols/colors for each suit, and create a new card design for each card in the deck.

6. Create a new card game, complete with card designs, symbols, colors and rules. Decide how many cards are in the deck, and how many players are needed to play the game. Teach your family and friends how to play the game.

7. Create a set of runes (small "stones" for "fortune telling" - about 1" x 1.5", or whatever size you wish). Use your own personal set of symbols. Decorate any way you wish. Be sure to cover the "stones" with some sort of protectant if you use cardboard or matboard. Create a booklet to go along with the "stones" so you can identify meanings quickly. Remember to create a "reverse" interpretation for each "stone". Teach someone else how to use them.

8. Make it small. Using just 1-inch-square blocks, make tiny images (called "inchies", due to their size). Keep them simple, but fill a large piece of matboard with them. Do one each day, using whatever color(s), subject(s), medium, etc. you like. If you use archival acid-free materials, you can keep the final pieces, have them framed, and keep them for years. Just one 20" x 16" matboard will provide 320 1-inch squares! Or you can give away the small bits of art to random people, or leave them in random places to be found by some stranger (*a la* Terry Border, of the Bent Objects blog and book fame). Be sure to sign/date the backs.

9. Learn a new technique, then write your own tutorial on how to achieve a similar result. Then learn another and do the same thing. And another. Wash, rinse, repeat. Don't just copy someone else's tutorial word for word, though. That would be bad karma. Use the methods that you've learned to create new and interesting work.

10. Design the perfect wardrobe, something that you would wear every day for any occasion. Start with the basics, then explore other, wilder, crazier options. Only design things you would actually wear, not what passes for "fashion". Don't forget active wear (if you are physically active), or sleep wear (if you wear anything while you sleep), and remember to include something for super-formal or super-casual occasions or events. Design one item per session.

11. Design a series of motivational posters. Make sure the background reflects a concept in the text, or at least allows the text to show up clearly. Use quotes from famous Creatives

(bonus points: use your own words!), but create your own backgrounds, using photos, drawings, paintings or images of other works you create. Make them large enough that you could actually get them printed for sale.

12. Design a series of greeting cards for all occasions, or blank notecards. Use the same ideas as in #11 above, or make up new ones.

13. Make a series of mini-paintings (between 2" x 2" and 5" x 5"). Use whatever medium you choose, but make them all related in subject, theme, color or mood. If you use a digital medium, print them out and mount them on small pieces of matboard. Sell or give them away, or keep them if you prefer.

14. Create a template using specific shapes, lines, etc. Using only this as a starting point, find as many ways to make this into "art" as you can. The template itself can be any size or shape, but I recommend a plain white background with gray or black lines that create the different areas of the template. Fill in as many or few of the areas with different colors and/or patterns as you like. Add or subtract design areas within the piece. Be as wild or sedate as you like. Turn the template, so it's oriented in different ways.

15. Create a set of symmetrical designs for filling in with different colors and/or patterns. Make it as simple or complex as you like. Use it as a set of templates that can be used (as in #14 above). Feel free to use kaleidoscope-making software or other techniques to aid in creating the symmetry.

16. Create a series of pictures that combine parts of one animal with parts of another. Be as detailed as possible. Try using puns for

inspiration (ex: horsefly, spider monkey, catfish, birddog...). This is an excellent way to experiment with collage.

17. Create a series of pictures inspired by whatever nature is doing outside your creative space. This doesn't necessarily mean you need to depict the day's weather, but that is also an option. If the day is foggy, you might use grays and pastels in your piece. If it is sunny and warm, you might choose a warmer palette, filled with reds, oranges, yellows and burnt umber. Move away from the obvious. Or toward it, if you'd rather.

18. Make a series of magnified drawings *a la* Georgia O'Keefe. Find a subject, then create a series of extreme closeups of that subject. If the subject is large enough, and you have enough images of it (ex: if you can take your own photos of it), you could theoretically create hundreds of large closeups of that one subject. If you own a decent camera with an excellent resolution and macro lens, feel free to try photographing the object instead.

19. Take your favorite poem, song lyric, quote, bible verse, curse (word or phrase, or even "fleas of a thousand camels" type curse) etc., and create an image to go with it. If one isn't enough, make a series based on similar word pictures. Or use the Top 40 songs as your prompt: use whatever song is at #1 for the moment, but don't repeat it. The next one should be the new #1 song, unless it's the same one as before, in which case use the #2 song, then the #3 song, and so on, until the lineup changes and you can select a different #1 or #2 song. Even if you hate the song. Do the series for as long as you can stand it.

20. Design as many water vehicles as you can imagine. Design the perfect fishing boat. If you don't fish, ask someone who does what it should look like, and what features it should have. Next, design the perfect personal watercraft. Next, how about the perfect floating car? Or houseboat? What else floats on water? Or runs beneath the surface?

21. Design a series of images of what you think the future will look like. Think of the basic needs: homes, clothing, food, transportation, leisure activities, birthing centers, death and mourning facilities, healing centers, gardens, walking paths, vehicle "paths", etc.... Is the future clean? Dirty? "Futuristic"? "Primitive"?

22. Design a series of magickal implements – the kind of things you might find in the shops along the streets of Diagon Ally, or within the walls of Merlin's laboratory. Remember: anything can hold magick! Anything at all...

23. Draw a series of body parts. Think small: eye, ear, nose, lips, toes... No need to draw an entire human being. Unless you decide to do so. Or maybe just once in a while. Your choice.

24. Draw a series of interlocking gears and pulleys. Use different sizes of gears that will mesh and turn other gears.

25. Draw a series of "Fruit of the Day" images. Cut any fruit in different ways. Put several pieces together into different types of containers. Draw single whole fruits, sliced fruits, several whole fruits in different bowls or plates, rotten fruit, fruit cut into chunks, cooked fruit, different varieties of the same fruit... When you run out of fruit, try vegetables.

26. Channel your inner Dali, and draw

"impossible" things, and things that don't make sense. These images can be dreamlike, or more "architectural", such as in M. C. Escher's work. Perhaps start with a "moebius strip" and go from there.

27. Draw a series of images based on the word "wonderland", whatever that means to you. It doesn't have to represent the famous story featuring Alice, the Hatter, the Red Queen, or anyone else in that universe, but it can if you want.

28. Draw a series of flowers. They can be real flowers or imaginary ones. They can be bold and bright or pastel and delicate. If you can, go visit a botanical garden of some sort and take as many photos as possible, from as many angles as possible, of as many different flowers as possible. Or use the Internet, and find photos of common, uncommon and/or rare, exotic flowers from all over the world. Create bizarre shapes, colors and patterns for imaginary flowers.

29. Develop a series of logos, symbols or emblems based on your name or your initials (1 or more). Give each a specific "feel" - formal, business, friendly, cute, loud, subtle, technical, rustic, futuristic, etc. - with its own shape, style and color palette. Make as many different versions as you can. Think outside the box. Incorporate your interests, likes, the seasons, moon phases, fonts, shapes, activities... Anything you can think of.

30. Design your perfect retirement home, the place where you will live once you no longer need to go to a "job" to earn your living (think about having won a *huge* lottery, one where, no matter how much you or your children

spend, your grandchildren will never need to worry about working at a fast-food restaurant, unless they want to – money is not an issue here). Be sure to include size, location, transportation arrangements, communication methods, number/type of rooms, design of furnishings, amenities, color scheme(s), work spaces (if any), special features (think solar panels, beverage dispensers, central vacuum system, intercom, Internet wiring, vehicle(s) and storage for same, storage/closets, laundry service, maid service, food service, groundskeeping service, pool service...), climate control (interior and/or exterior), etc. Design one room or system at a time, and be sure that each room/system functions properly with the rest of the home. Also remember to design the furniture that will be in and around the home (in case you decide to have some outdoor rooms as well). Be as detailed as possible, especially with color, material and patterns.

40 More Prompts

Here are a bonus set of single-word prompts to help you jumpstart that Creative Muse hiding deep inside your mind. Perhaps one or more of these will speak to her, and wake her up. Try picking two at random, and see what happens.

1. Dream
2. Haunted
3. Memory
4. Secret
5. Promise
6. Moonlight
7. Whisper
8. Regrets
9. Lies
10. Revenge
11. Midnight
12. Beauty
13. Echo
14. Alone
15. Letters
16. Addiction
17. Trust
18. Temptation
19. Together
20. Fearless
21. Time
22. Obsession
23. Mirror
24. Taboo
25. Dust
26. Sword

The Beginning

That's right: "the beginning", not "the end", because you now have another very powerful tool to keep your creativity going strong for as long as you wish. So consider today the beginning of a new era for your creative pursuits.

Well, there you have it: 100 More Ways to Boost Your Creativity. This is not meant to be an exhaustive list of all the ways you can break through a temporary block. In fact, I'm sure you can come up with at least another 100 ways yourself.

I'd love to hear how this little guide helped you. Email me with your thoughts at:
Guide@SerendipityMuse.com.

And once again, thank you for walking the creative path with me for a little while. I've enjoyed our time together, and hope you have, too. Here's to us Creatives!

About the Author

Lisa Mayfield has been creating in one form or another since she could hold a crayon, often to her mother's chagrin. Creativity has been an obsession for her throughout her life as she has worked in various media, from drawing and sculpting, to fiber arts and costume design, to writing and web design. She is a slave to her Muse and prefers whichever medium her Muse tells her to use. She is often neglected by her Muse for days or weeks at a time. It's usually about that time that Ms. Muse comes back around and bonks her on the head with more ideas than she can possibly explore in a lifetime.

Lisa has a day job, a husband, 4 children (2 still at home), 3 dogs, and a house that constantly complains about being neglected. She doesn't like to cook or clean, but enjoys eating and making messes. When she isn't being creative, she's probably dreaming about being creative. She always has at least a dozen projects in various stages of progress, from early planning to almost completed. This guide is her second published work. Her website is **SerendipityMuse.com**. Why not stop by for a visit?

www.ingramcontent.com/pod-product-compliance
Lightning Source LLC
Chambersburg PA
CBHW071548170526
45166CB00004B/1587